PET GALLERY

FUR BABIES

ILLUSTRATED BY PATRICK SULLIVAN

Published in 2016 by: Spirit Marketing, LLC
700 Broadway Boulevard, Suite 101, Kansas City, MO 64105

hellospiritmarketing.com
© 2016 Spirit Marketing

ISBN: 978-0-9965998-7-0

Designed in Kansas City by Chris Evans, Patrick Sullivan, and Chris Simmons.

For information about custom editions, special sales, and premium and corporate purchases, please contact Spirit Marketing at info@hellospiritmail.com or 1.888.288.3972.

Printed 4/16-5/16 in USA

**Find more ways
to color your happiness at
handcraftedcoloring.com**

Patrick Sullivan

A multi-disciplined artist based in Kansas City who specializes in printmaking, drawing, collage, illustration, and design. Patrick's diverse career in fashion, advertising, and product development has made him the perfect artist to create this unique title. His passion for all things design started early, and his eagerness to inspire others with his work is still a driving force. A Kansas State University graduate with a Bachelor of Fine Art degree, Patrick's work has been featured in galleries all over the world, and retail shelves across America.

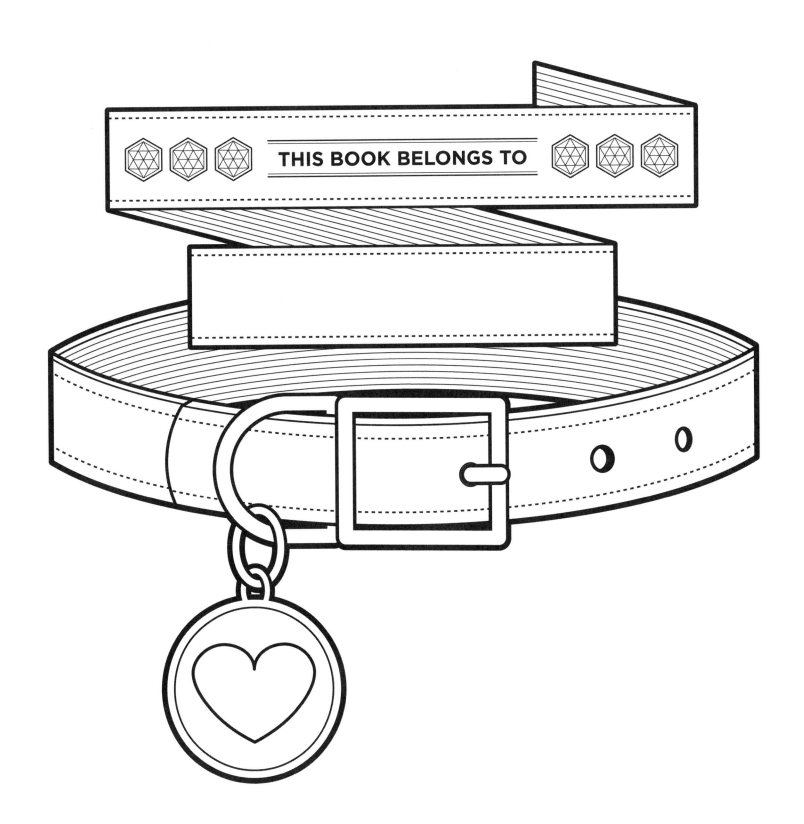

THIS BOOK BELONGS TO

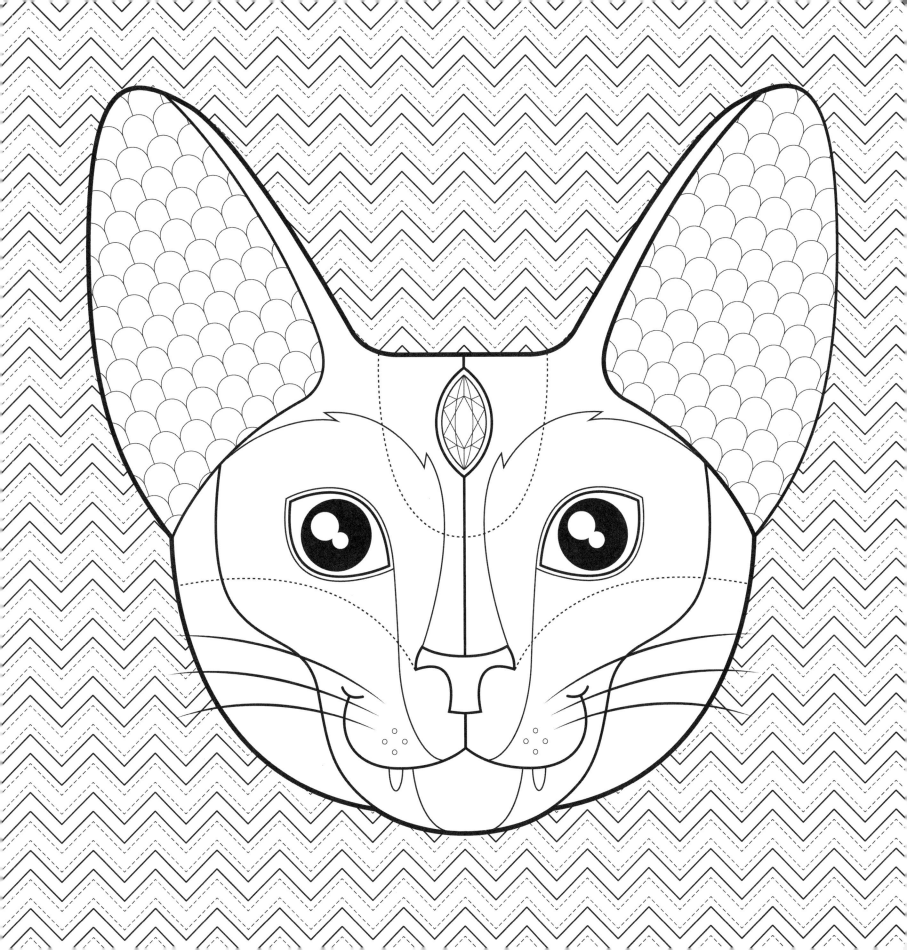

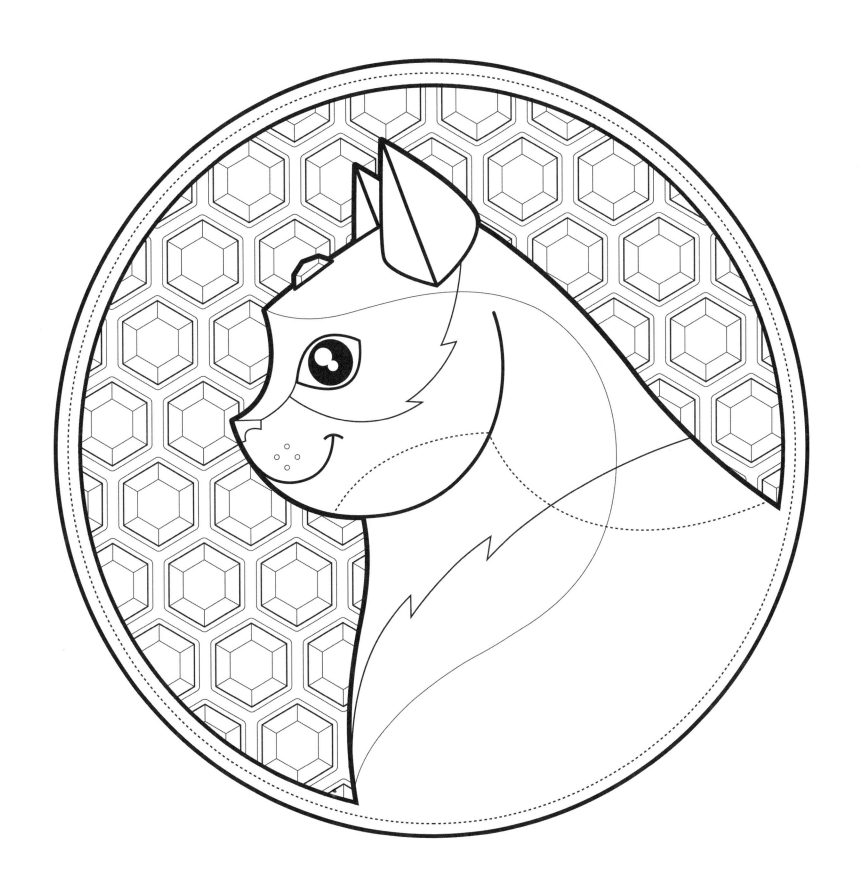

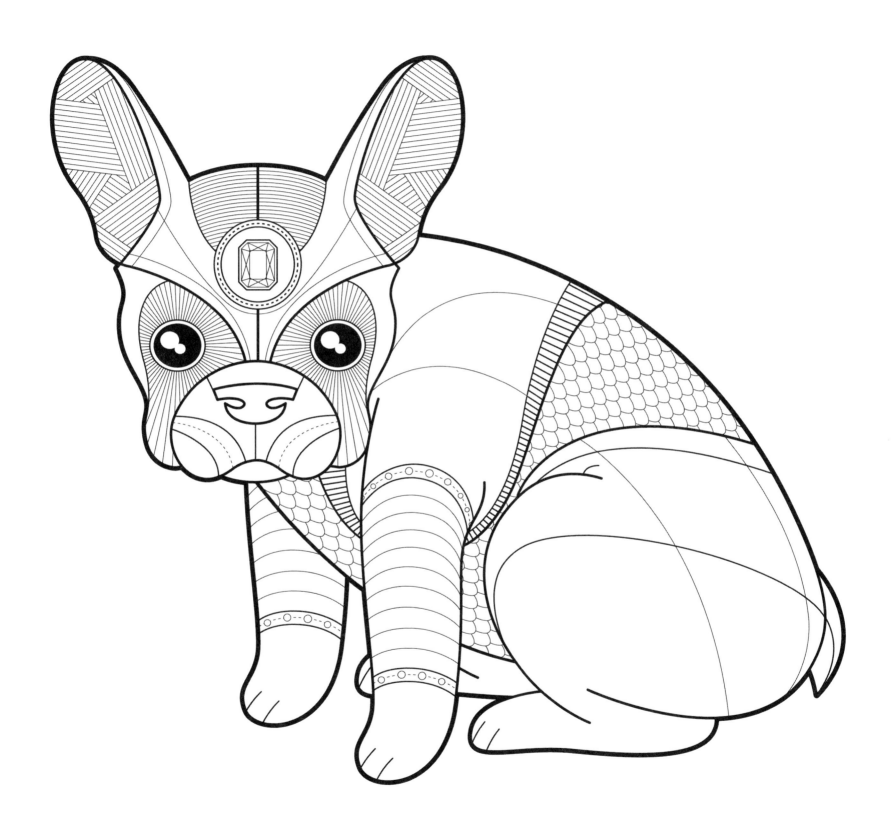

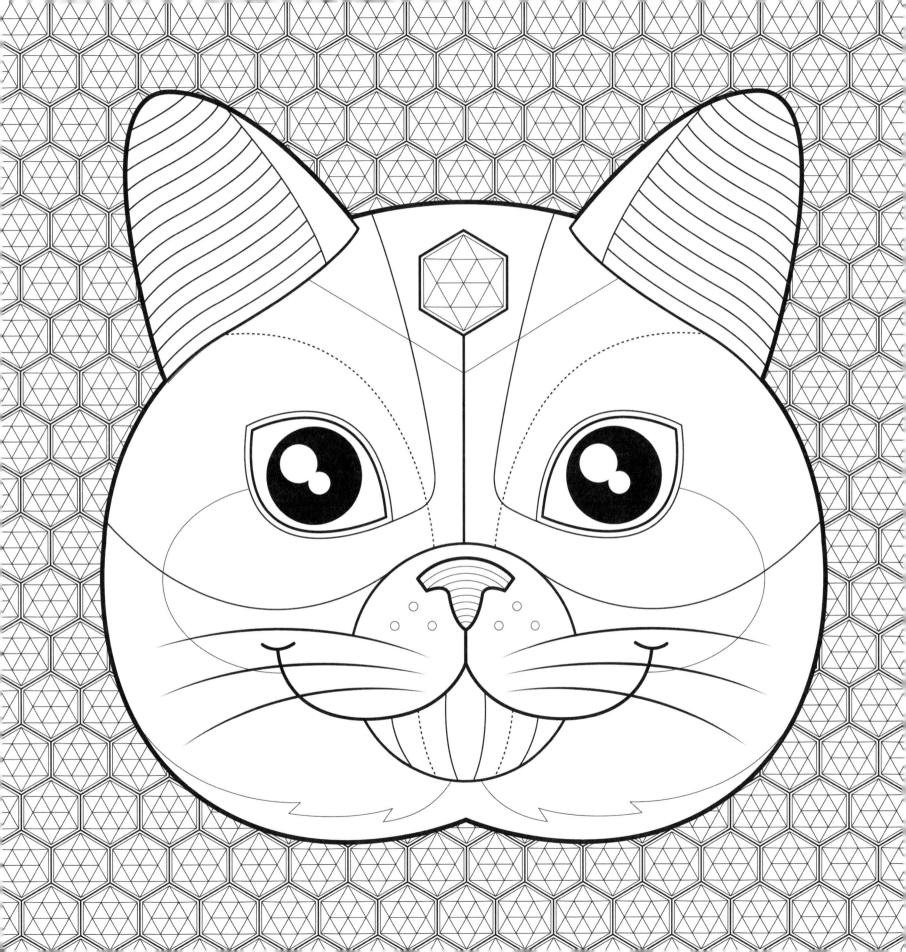

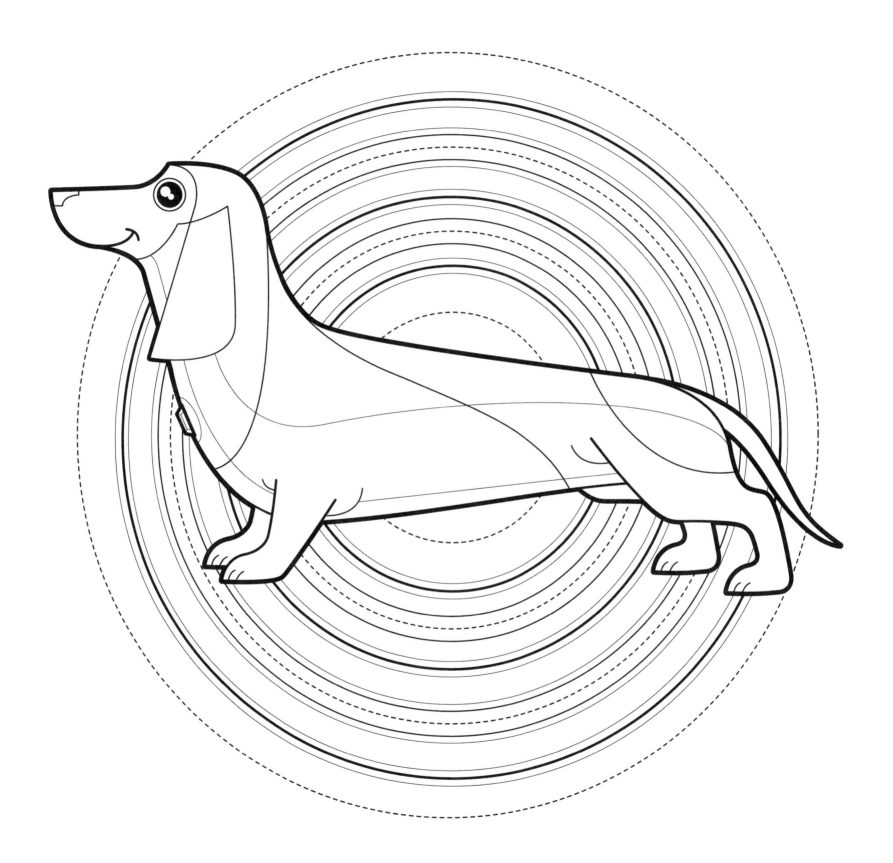

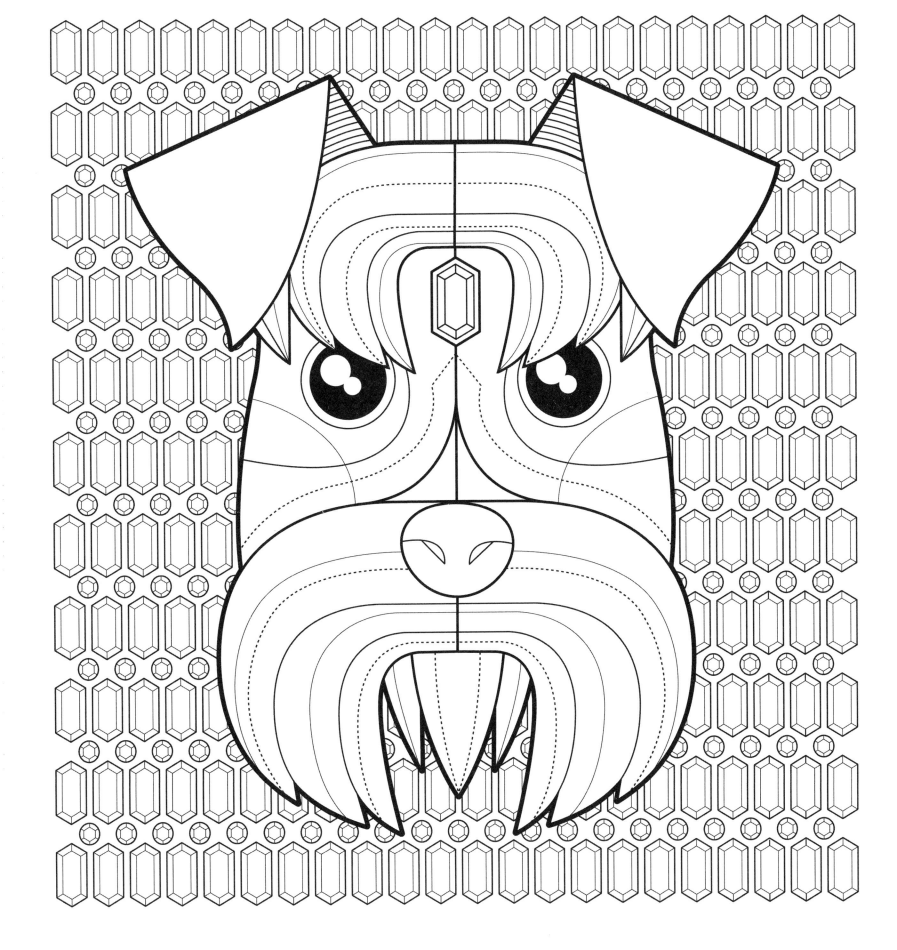

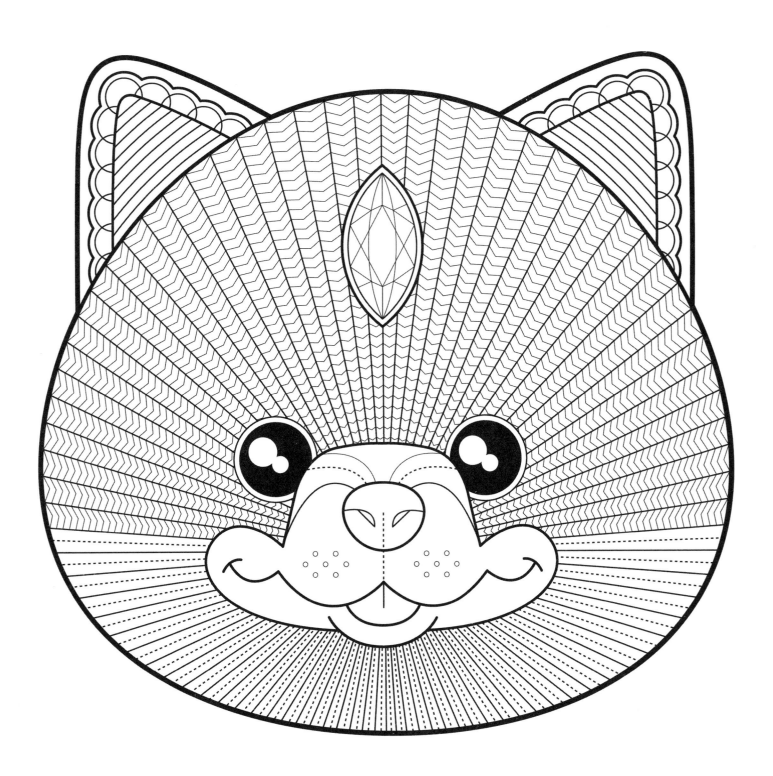

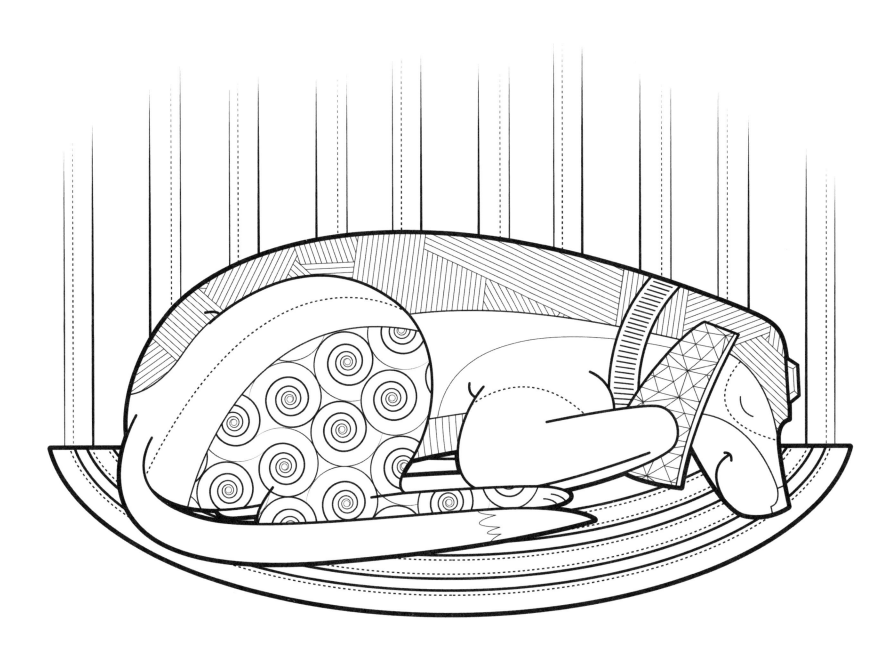